THE PATRON

THE PATRON

Antonia Rachel Ward

QUERENCIA

Querencia Press – Chicago IL

QUERENCIA PRESS

ISBN 978 1 959118 92 3

Cover Art: Emily Perkovich
Photo of Dress from the Alexander McQueen
Spring/Summer 2017 Paris Fashion Week Show

·

www.querenciapress.com

First Published in 2024

Querencia Press, LLC
Chicago IL

Printed & Bound in the United States of America

ALSO BY ANTONIA RACHEL WARD

Marionette
Attack of the Killer Tumbleweeds
DreamScape

Dedicated to the memory of Lee Alexander McQueen.

Thank you for the inspiration.

contents

i: (con)fusion

it starts
(as things often do)
in a nightclub
a place of potential, of mingling
bodies, familiar and unfamiliar faces, the lingering
scents of perfume and aftershave,
cigarette smoke
and sweat

torsos fused on the dance floor—
flailing limbs, grasping fingers,
hungry mouths

a many-headed monster,
stitched together with lust and abandonment,
looking for nothing more
than to get wasted
and forget

ii: home

...forget *her*

he swirls
in the midst of the maelstrom
bloodstream burning with alcohol—
a necessary fire,
obliterating all that came before

forget her

her memory is an arrhythmia jarring
the music's pulse—
clutching at him
indiscriminate

forget her

a stop of breath
a glimpse in a stranger's eyes
an echo

isabella

she has lodged in his brain,
a siphonophore's sting
venomous, even after death

head spinning, he stumbles outside,
into freezing sea air

lured by her siren song

the stars overhead are bright
—too bright—
the pier flashes neon colours,
ferris wheel whirling a queasy dance

but he looks only to the sea—
its black expanse,
the lap of the waves against the beach

and her song, calling him
home.

iii: memento mori

star-strewn night
crystal clear and soundless,
save for the soft lap of the waves
against the beach

somehow
the city he just left
seems an eternity away

he sits,
hands sinking into wet sand,
breath steaming,
sea licking at his toes

water surges,
a sudden wave of foam
covering him to the waist, leaving in its wake—

like driftwood—

a woman,
head haloed by the silver of the full moon

isabella

she wears the ocean itself—
sea foam enveloping her body in an oyster swirl,
hair wet and seaweed-like,
mascara-black trails
running down her cheeks

come with me

he takes her outstretched hand
and she pulls him into the surf

waist deep

chest deep

—this is the end—

until he is

submerged

completely,
water pouring over his head,
and she is swimming,
pulling him down

deeper

deeper

deeper

iv: platonic

there is no way forward

he sinks
beneath the skin of consciousness
into the hot, molten core
of love
stamped—
like a brand on the heart

do you remember me yet?

but who can remember a whole soul?
its infinite complexity,
kaleidoscopic detail—
the fractal repeating patterns
of life,
experience,
dreams, etched upon its surface
like the delicate markings
of butterfly wings
and just as easily erased

*do you remember
what you did to me?*

she returns to him in snapshots—
their first meeting, when she burned like the sun,
the way she'd kissed him on both cheeks with every
greeting,

the times she'd called him, drunk and crying,
the last time—

so many polaroids, frittered away
meaningless currency,
until one day,
she was gone

there is no way forward

only back,
sinking deeper into memory,
to the beginning—
to the moment
of creation

v: creation

you were born in blood
and it was i who birthed you

i split apart,
slashed up my middle with the swoosh
of knife slicing through silk,
and you came forth
to stalk your victims

you were beautiful,
talented—
golden
in my eyes,
and you wrapped your barbed-wire tendrils around my
heart,
squeezing until it hurt

i am your mother,
your lover,
your sister,
your friend

i lifted you
from the dark womb of obscurity
and held you to the light
to be worshipped
to be adored

i did not cut the cord

i kept you tied to me,
my blood your blood
my food your sustenance
until you were strong enough to walk alone and then—

i made you drag me with you,
basking in your reflected glory
clinging to my bloody rope

i made you

you are mine

iv: ripper

he began in the city,
electric light spilling from boundaried panes,
each window a picture frame
onto a life confined within four walls

night by foggy night, he walked
concrete-slabbed pavements—
the swoosh of passing cars,
red brake-lights reflected in rain,
puddles mirroring black sky

he knew the corners where whores waited,
shining apples, ready to be plucked,
the alleyways ripe for a late-night assignation
the rotten, the dismissed, the ignored—
his kin

but he'd always known his roots ran deeper,
snaking between the cracks in the concrete,
plunging into the earth itself,
searching for something solid,
ancient,
lasting

a tether

he tried to trace his ancestry—
placed his palm to the soil
and felt the earth split,
revealing its secrets

whispering of histories long past:
wildness and romance,
passion and fury,
and their one constant—
pain

the inevitability of loss,
of loneliness,
and the certainty that beauty
would one day
die

vii: bloom

take this blossom,
flush in its fledgling bloom:
this is you—
this is how i saw you first

dew-fresh,
newly budded,
petals opening as you turned towards the sun
r e a c h i n g

i wanted you

to press your velvet softness to my lips
and revive me

breathe life back into my crumpled years
arresting
the slow dissolution of entropy

everything i had wasted
you still had to come

i could buy an armful of you—
feed you, water you,
lovingly arrange you in a vase

and watch you wilt

viii: sanctuary

he built a room around his heart
the day his father left

a perfect copy of his own—
peeling posters tacked onto walls,
paint flaking from the doorframe,
black mould climbing the walls

a sanctuary

he folded himself up tight
like origami paper
and tucked himself away

hidden,
small,

safe

until isabella came
and he felt her basilisk gaze
look through his walls
—through his heart—
and see
him

he unfolded, just a little—
just enough
that she could open his door,

and slip
right
in

ix: invader

tell me your dreams, child
those creations that seduce you—
feverish, deep-core imaginings,
in the thickness of night

tell them to me—
let me examine their soft
petal edges, fragile colour
staining eager fingers

let me dart my probing tongue
into their damp, dark centres
sweet nectar of submerged
desires wet on my lips

let me wrap myself in their folds
cocoon-like, entangling my fibres
with yours until you no longer know
how to unravel us

i am a part of you now
the soul of your organism
coated in your juices and you
will not forget me

x: vulture

she was hollywood—
old school glamour,
red lips,
cinched waist,
voice curling from her throat
like smoke

and he—
he was on the floor
kissing her louboutins,
entranced by that red-blood sole

he offered himself
like a banquet,
for her to dine on—
sharp-beaked,
paring flesh from bone

throwing his scraps to her children,
who gulped them down
—red throated, shrieking—
and screamed for more

a shred of muscle here,
an eyeball there,
until he was picked clean,
no more than bones
bleaching in the sun's fire

and she took flight,
circling overhead,

out of reach

xi: pride

pride defines your boundary—
a border, shell-like,
encircling your embryonic self

it is a hard casing, but brittle—
easily cracked,
difficult to repair

with gentle fingers, i probe the fractures—
you recoil,
nursing your wounds

at those moments, cornered,
you flare with rage,
reducing me to ash

yet you are at your most fearsome
when you slough your shell off completely
and stand naked and vulnerable
daring me to do the same

that's when i want to tell you
i love you

but i can't.

xii: freak show

roll up, roll up!
the circus is in town!

we have it all,
ladies and gentlemen,
so prepare to be entertained

laugh!
at the clown in his oversized clothes
pretending to be a real boy

scream!
at the fearsome woman-vulture,
light glinting off her bloody talons

lose yourself!
in the hall of endless mirrors
and forget which face is yours

gape!
at the conjoined souls
as they battle to share—

one heart
one lung
one bloodstream

turn away in horror!
as they consume
each other

xiii: starlight

starlight, you called her
a heavenly haze—
insubstantial as gas and dust

into my earthly body of decaying cells,
you tried to breathe her galactic glow,
and stood back, admiring how
she burned, white hot,
singeing me at the edges

i could not hold her—
her stellar energy expanded,
consuming my all-too-corporeal mass

i was only human, after all
afflicted by the inevitable
disintegration
of entropy

beneath a celestial weight,
your fantasy collapsed into me

just me, a woman
who will one day fade
to dust

xiv: proserpine

i do not remember when
i swallowed the seed,
only the sensation of it
sour and unsatisfying
slipping down my throat.

it lodged in my chest,
flowering tumorous
accumulations
beneath smooth skin,
beginning a slow rot.

you spectate
as i eat myself,
consuming my own
bilious sweetness,
product of aeons
of decay.

i am the underworld.
a sublime mistress,
source of fascination
and fear.

you might hold me—
at arm's length.

you might worship me—
from a distance.

but when I surface
in the springtime,
black with decay,
vomiting feelings,
and crawling with putrefaction—

you will not let me near.

xv: the tailor

they wanted him—
isabella's children,
hungry gannets with their red throats

tired of throwing trinkets
into a hole they could never fill,
they craved what only he could give them
(or so they believed)

authenticity

whisper it! the word deserves
a reverent hush

desperate to imbibe
some of his promise,
they stripped his bones clean,
and isabella,
—the hungriest of them all—
burrowed inside his ribcage
and ate his heart, too

they sat his grinning corpse
on a gilded throne,
placed a paper crown
upon his head

paraded him through the streets like a beggar-king,
a curiosity—
the poor boy turned genius

look how it talks
it could almost be human!

they wore his skin like gowns
and his gowns like skin

and while they tried to inhabit him, he—

retreated

into the secret interior room,
which had once been his sanctuary
before he had let isabella in—
before she watched from every shadow,
lurked in every corner

nowhere was safe
from thoughts of her,
honey-sweet
but poisonous

and so he recast her,
in the quiet of that secret workshop—
unstitched her limb by limb
and sewed her back together
in his own image—

a monstrosity
a freak

like him

his handiwork complete,
he held her up for her hungry children to see
and they laughed
and laughed
and laughed

xvi: ugly

turn the mirror upon yourself,
isabella
don't wince
don't cower—
face its cruel reflection
head on

how does it feel
to fall?
to watch your children turn on you,
your own creation betray you?

you chose to be a shining sun,
a central point in a world enraptured
by beauty, and they,
blinded by your light,
were too dazzled to see the truth

but age
makes fools of us all
and your glamour has worn thin
they see you for what you are,

isabella

what you always were—

ridiculous
contemptible

ugly

xvii: mercury

revolve—
ancient messenger
swift-winged feet flying
circling clockwork

revolve—
orbital gears grind
groove riven in gold
perpetual spin

revolve—
surrendered to scorching sun
surface split by scars
pressure rising

revolve—
quicksilver settling
madness accumulating
incremental poison

revolve—

xviii: cleave

take your tailor's scissors
and snip away,
carefully paring
flesh from bone
heart from heart

where once we were conjoined
now we are two

how does it feel
to be alone?

xix: reflection

sometimes, there are moments like these
moments that score a line

down the centre of your life
like a knife cutting through cloth—

this is before,
this is after.

the before—

the weight of her
pressing on his chest

cancelled calls
unanswered messages

the need to be free
a searing itch in his veins

you're nothing without me

but he had to be
something

didn't he?

had to find a way to fill his own skin
without her

the after—

he looked for himself
in her children's eyes

a thousand mirror-images,
and none of them was him

xx: annihilation

do you remember me now?

she coils around him,
eel-like and slippery in her watery grave—
hair swimming with seaweed
eyes shining like black pearls

now, in her coral palace
in the darkest depths,
she reveals her true form,
her sea-ruined corpse
bloated and grinning

do you remember me now?

she was creation
and annihilation
his maker—
and his destroyer

he clings to her,
sea filling his lungs

do you remember me now?
do you remember me?
do you?
now?

afterword

The Patron was a truly freeing experience to write. The idea started off as a planned novelette, about a young, talented working-class designer drawn into a toxic co-dependency with his wealthy patron, Isabella. But something about the story asked for a looser, more metaphorical approach than prose could provide, and eventually I settled on the notion of writing a linked series of poems conveying the back-and-forth of the two characters' relationship. In this I tried to convey some of my impressions about class and wealth, the role of art in the modern world, and the twisting of authenticity into a commodity that can be bought and sold. I would like to extend a huge thank you to Querencia Press and Emily Perkovich for giving me the opportunity to bring this book to life.

Many of these poems were directly inspired by collections designed by Alexander McQueen, and the book *Alexander McQueen: Savage Beauty* was my constant companion as I wrote. If anyone is interested to look the collections up, they are as follows:

"memento-mori" — "Oyster" Dress, *Irere*, spring / summer 2003
"platonic" — *Plato's Atlantis*, spring / summer 2010
"creation"— *Jack the Ripper Stalks His Victims*, MA Graduation Collection, 1992
"ripper" — *Highland Rape*, autumn / winter 1995-96 and *Widows of Culloden*, autumn / winter 2006-7
"bloom" — *Sarabande*, spring / summer 2007
"vulture" — *The Horn of Plenty*, autumn / winter 2009-10
"freak show" — *It's Only a Game*, spring / summer 2005
"proserpine" and "ugly" — *VOSS*, spring / summer 2001
"the tailor" — *No. 13*, spring / summer 1999
"annihilation" — *Highland Rape*, autumn / winter 1995-96

notes on previous publications

"proserpine" — First published in *Under Her Skin* by Blackspot Books, April 2022.

"invader", "starlight" — First published in *Not Ghosts But Spirits Vol. II* by Querencia Press, April 2023.